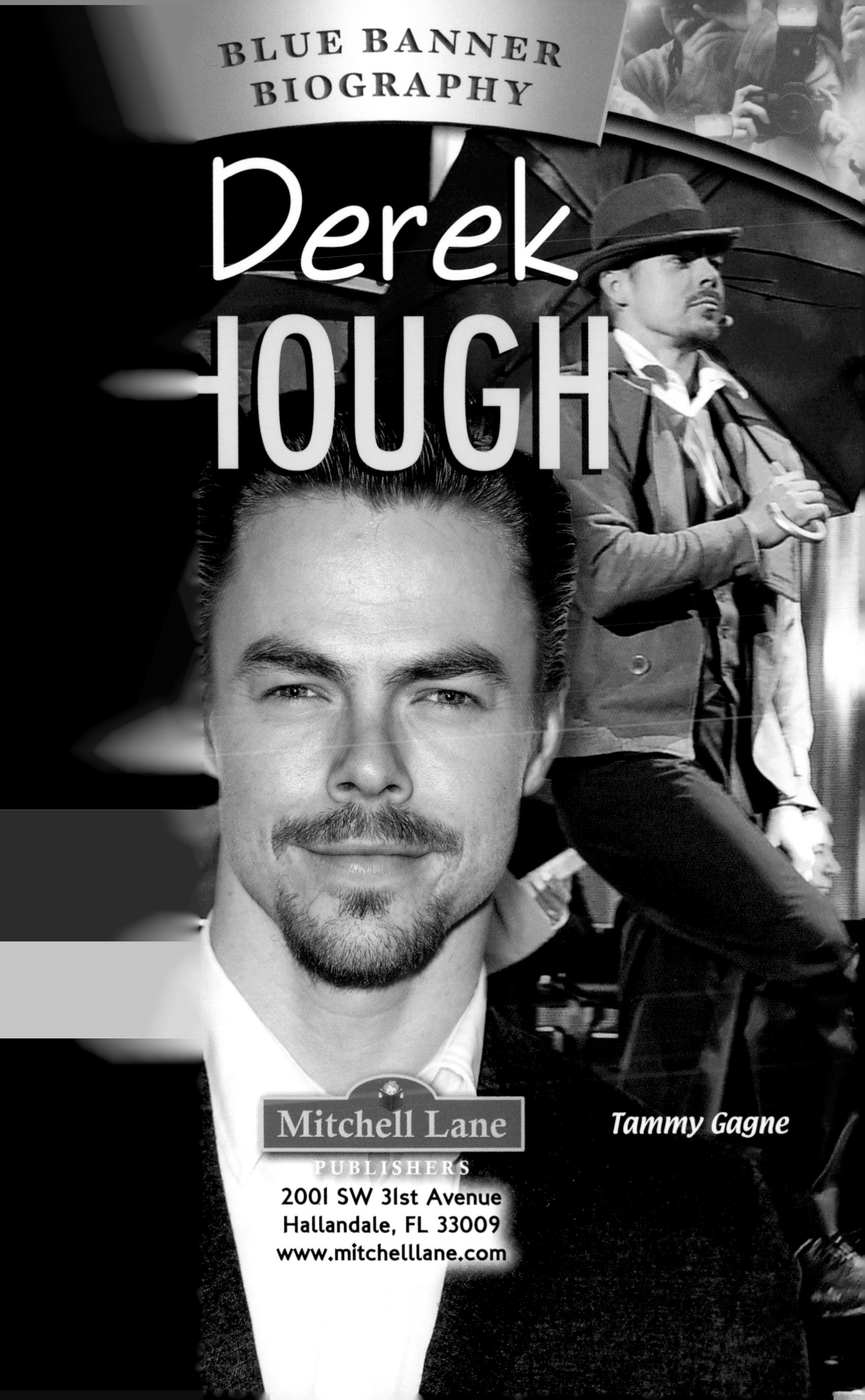

BLUE BANNER
BIOGRAPHY

Derek
HOUGH

Tammy Gagne

Mitchell Lane
PUBLISHERS

2001 SW 31st Avenue
Hallandale, FL 33009
www.mitchelllane.com

Printing   1   2   3   4   5   6   7   8   9

Blue Banner Biographies

Library of Congress Cataloging-in-Publication Data
Names: Gagne, Tammy, author.
Title: Derek Hough / by Tammy Gagne.
Description: Hallandale, FL : Mitchell Lane Publishers, [2018] | Series: Blue banner biographies | Includes bibliographical references and index.
Identifiers: LCCN 2017024467 | ISBN 9781680201185 (library bound)
Subjects: LCSH: Hough, Derek, 1985– —Juvenile literature. | Ballroom dancers—United States— Biography—Juvenile literature. | Choreographers—United States—Biography—Juvenile literature.
Classification: LCC GV1785.H67 G33 2018 | DDC 793.3/3092 [B] —dc23
LC record available at https://lccn.loc.gov/2017024467

eBook ISBN: 978-1-68020-119-2

ABOUT THE AUTHOR: Tammy Gagne is the author of numerous books for adults and children, including *Ed Sheeran* and *The Weeknd* for Mitchell Lane Publishers. She resides in northern New England with her husband and son. One of her favorite pastimes is visiting schools to speak to kids about the writing process.

PUBLISHER'S NOTE: The following story has been thoroughly researched and to the best of our knowledge represents a true story. While every possible effort has been made to ensure accuracy, the publisher will not assume liability for damages caused by inaccuracies in the data and makes no warranty on the accuracy of the information contained herein. This story has not been authorized or endorsed by Derek Hough.

Blue Banner Biography

Derek Hough and Bindi Irwin danced all the way to the Dancing with the Stars *season finale in 2015. Derek and Bindi kept going strong as each of the other couples were eliminated in the weekly competition. In November, the pair won the famed mirror ball trophy.*

CHAPTER 1

Those Who Can, Teach

*C*onfetti rained down on Bindi Irwin and Derek Hough as their fellow *Dancing with the Stars* cast members hoisted the newly named winners onto their shoulders. The live audience in Los Angeles cheered. Millions of television viewers also celebrated the popular television show's season finale in December 2015.

Derek, the professional dancer of the pair, had taught a variety of dances to the 17-year-old daughter of famous Australian wildlife conservationist Steve Irwin. Like the other dancers, they performed one each week. The show's judges assigned scores to each couple's performance. Viewers then weighed in on which couple should be **eliminated** that week. For Bindi and Derek, that elimination never came.

Being the professional half of the dancing couple is not easy. Although some celebrity contestants have dance experience, most have never performed on a stage. Likewise, some contestants are naturals when it comes to dance, while others find it much more challenging. Irwin fell into the latter category on both counts. As they headed into the final weeks of the competition, Derek revealed to the *Daily Mail* that she had struggled in the beginning. "No joke, she could not dance, she really couldn't."

This is where the pro's talent for teaching and the **amateur** contestant's hard work come into the picture. "I knew Bindi had this dancer living inside of her that she just wanted to get out," Derek continued. He didn't take the credit for their success, though. "I'll give her the steps and I'll give her the moves and she's doing them and technique, and it's working hard on that," he added. "But then something else happens that she does and it's just all her. And it's this performance, it's this connection, it's this commitment to the steps. It's teachable, but it's only teachable to a certain degree . . . she goes beyond that."

> Derek's win with Bindi Irwin was his sixth. He is the only professional dancer to win the competition that many times.

Derek's win with Bindi Irwin was his sixth. He is the only professional dancer to win the competition that many times. He shared these victories with such big names as *Dirty Dancing* star Jennifer Grey, *Glee* actress Amber Riley, and country music singer Kellie Pickler.

Dancing runs in the Hough family. Derek's sister Julianne is also a professional dancer. Like her big brother, she has frequently appeared on *Dancing with the Stars*. She has also served as a judge for the show. The Houghs even tour together. Their 2016 *Move Live on Tour* sold out in so many cities around the United States that they decided to

In Season 11 of Dancing with the Stars, *Derek was paired with* Dirty
Dancing *star Jennifer Grey. They performed a sample from one of their
winning dance routines on* Good Morning America *on November 24,
2010.*

tour again the following year with *Move Beyond Live on Tour*.

According to their father, Bruce Hough, the siblings have been dancing since they could walk. "Our home videos are pretty self-evident that these kids loved to shake, rattle, and roll," he told *People* magazine.

In addition to dancing, Derek is an actor who has appeared in television, movies, and stage productions.

Derek and his sister Julianne are seen here performing in the Move Live on Tour *show at the Durham Performing Arts Center in North Carolina.*

Even then, though, dancing is often a big part of his roles. In the 2013 film *Make Your Move*, for example, Derek played Donny, a young man who makes his living dancing on the street. In a London production of *Footloose: The Musical*, a play about a town that has banned music and dancing, Derek played Ren. He fights to change the harsh rule. And in 2016, he appeared in NBC's musical production *Hairspray Live!*

In 2014, he added book authorship to his list of accomplishments. His **memoir**, *Taking the Lead: Lessons from a Life in Motion*, became a *New York Times* Best Seller. Derek wrote, "I want variety in my life; I like my days filled with new and different things. I love exploring the world, meeting new people, learning new crafts and art. It's why you might often read what I'm up to and scratch your head. 'I didn't know Derek did that.' I probably didn't before, but I do now."

Derek's book, Taking the Lead: Lessons from a Life in Motion, *made* The New York Times *Best Seller list.*

Derek donates his time to many important charities. In 2008, he attended the 15th annual Race to Erase MS event in Los Angeles with his mother Marianne and his sister Julianne.

An Active and Creative Child

Derek Hough was born on May 17, 1985 in Salt Lake City, Utah. His parents, Bruce and Marianne, met when they joined a ballroom dance team at Brigham Young University–Idaho. Music and dancing remained a regular part of life for the Houghs as the couple raised their five children. Derek has three older sisters—Sharee, Marabeth, and Katherine—while Julianne was born in 1988. "In my household, I had drums and bongos and guitars, and we were always just playing music and playing around," he said to *Backstage*. "I think I envisioned myself onstage and being a rock star—you know, playing music and rocking out and feeling the lights on me [in front of] thousands of people."

Derek was an active child, often using his imagination during playtime. He remembers that he and his sisters used the family's camcorder to make their own movies and commercials. Sometimes they would reenact scenes from their favorite films. Then he would watch himself in slow motion. He was fascinated by the way his body looked when he flipped in the air. At this point, though, he was more interested in mimicking moves from video games than dancing. He especially wanted to be a Teenage Mutant Ninja Turtle.

The Houghs encouraged their kids' creativity. One day young Derek told his mother he wanted a sword. Instead of buying one, she told him to draw it. Then she helped him make a toy sword out of wood to match the blade he had drawn. They even covered it with paint that glowed in the dark. Because his mother typically did things like this, Derek thought that his family was poor. It wasn't. His parents wanted their children to use their imaginations to create things instead of going to the store and buying them. This approach made them different from their neighbors.

> *Derek felt like he didn't belong—until the day his mother signed him up for a dance class. He quickly realized he had a natural talent.*

Derek was glad his family was different. But some kids in his neighborhood thought otherwise. They especially thought it was odd that a boy would like dancing so much. They used it as an excuse to pick on him, both in and out of school. For many years, Derek never told anyone about being bullied. Now he wishes he had reached out to someone—his parents, older sisters, teachers, or someone else—and explained what was going on.

As an adult, Derek began speaking out about bullying. The Gay, Lesbian, & Straight Education Network (GLSEN) is an organization that works to create safe schools for all students. In 2014, GLSEN honored Derek Hough with an award for his efforts. In his acceptance speech, he pointed out that this problem comes in many forms. "Bullying can be physical, **verbal**, or emotional," he explained. "Words and threats are just as painful as fists, especially with social media these days."

He extended his support for kids who are victims of bullying. "Let me tell you right now, you are not alone," he continued. And he offered advice to keep them from becoming bullies themselves. "You can work hard, gain friends and be a good person. [You can] be a tall beautiful skyscraper or you can tear down all the buildings around you to make yourself feel big even though you're not. That's what bullies do."

Derek found school difficult in more ways than one. He struggled with learning facts and figures. After a while he began feeling like he wasn't smart enough. He also didn't have many friends. He was on the smaller side and saw himself as **awkward**. He tried to fit in by showing how fast he could move while playing football at recess. But he always felt like he was different from the other kids. They didn't share or appreciate his fondness for creativity.

Derek felt like he didn't belong — until the day his mother signed him up for a dance class. He quickly realized he had a natural talent. Just as important, dancing allowed him to express all of his emotions through his movements on the dance floor. While young Derek did not know it yet, he had found something that would become much more than a hobby.

When Derek was honored at the 2016 Television Industry Advocacy Awards in West Hollywood, California, he brought his father Bruce to the event.

Learning and Growing

Derek began competing in ballroom dance competitions. His partner was Autumn DelGrosso, whom he met at his dance classes. They both still had much to learn about the **technical** moves of dances like the cha-cha, rumba, and samba.

But what they lacked in experience, they made up for in style. The creativity that Derek's parents had encouraged was paying off. During one competition, he noticed an audience member holding a bouquet of roses. Completely out of the blue, he raced into the crowd and snatched one of the flowers. He completed his dance with the rose between his teeth. The audience loved the personality he added to his performance.

Derek was learning that he could develop his talents and be himself at the same time. This combination made him stand out as a performer. People who simply went through the motions of dancing did not look like they were enjoying themselves. On the other hand, Derek thoroughly enjoyed making people smile, truly entertaining them. His passion for dance added to his self-confidence while he continued to master the steps and other technical movements.

Derek's drive also made him stand out among other dancers his age. It even motivated his young partner. Autumn realized that Derek was putting out a maximum effort every time they performed together. That inspired her to do the same thing so she could keep up with him.

Looking back on his education and career in dance, Derek realizes that many of his biggest opportunities presented themselves when he least expected them.

When Derek was 11, he found out his parents were getting divorced. Like many kids in this situation, he felt confused, sad, and angry. And he did not always know how to deal with these emotions. He began doing things he had never done before, such as skipping school. He even skipped his dance lessons. He hung out with the kids who behaved badly. He eventually realized he was trying to become someone else, someone tougher than he felt he really was. His poor choices were also probably a way of getting back at his parents.

Fortunately, his parents made sure that Derek and his sisters kept doing the things that brought them joy. During the divorce, his father even took him and Autumn on a trip to England for the Blackpool Dance Festival. Although they did not win any of their competitions on the trip, Derek came home with a renewed sense of purpose. He knew he wanted to dance more than anything. He also realized that he had a lot of work to do if he was going to make his dreams come true. Wasting his talents by skipping his dance classes wasn't going to get him anywhere.

It was around this time that world champion dancers Corky and Shirley Ballas came to teach at Derek's dance school. Shirley quickly noticed that Derek showed a great deal of passion and **potential** for dance. She also saw that he still was having problems dealing with his parents' divorce. When the couple prepared to return to their home in England, they offered to take Derek with them. By living with them, he could attend the Italia Conti Academy of Theatre Arts along with their son Mark. The school trained young people in many forms of dance, music, and theater. Derek and his parents discussed this amazing opportunity and decided to accept it. Julianne soon joined her big brother as she pursued her own dream of becoming a dancer. Along with Mark, the siblings formed a pop music trio called 2B1G ("2 Boys, 1 Girl.").

Looking back on his education and career in dance, Derek realizes that many of his biggest opportunities presented themselves when he least expected them. "I just took it and ran with it over the years. I haven't really planned a lot of the things that I've accomplished," he told *Backstage*. "There's that expression—[luck is what happens] when preparation meets opportunity. Sometimes you're prepared and there's no opportunity. Sometimes you have all the opportunities, but you're not prepared. I was always preparing for something and, luckily, when the opportunity came, even if I wasn't fully ready, I was ready to take it on."

In 2006, Derek played the lead role in the London production of Footloose: The Musical, *based on the popular movie* Footloose. *He is seen here dancing with fellow cast member Lorna Want.*

Conquering the Worlds

Derek kept competing after his move to London. He would have new partners and even more disappointments. Learning to perform his very best from start to finish took time. When he returned to the Blackpool Dance Festival, he was a bit older and had more experience. He thought he had an excellent chance of winning. By the end of his final performance, fans were even chanting the number he and his partner wore on their backs. But to his surprise and disappointment, another couple took the first prize.

After the competition, Derek asked the judges why he didn't win. One of them explained that he had won the last round but not the entire competition. Derek was used to giving 100 percent. Now, as Corky advised him, he needed to give 110 percent during each and every round.

With hard work and still more new partners, Derek began winning competitions in England, France, and Italy. In 2003, he even became a world champion when he and Aneta Piotrowska won the Blackpool Under-21 Latin Championships.

Winning this top honor felt great—for a while. Soon Derek realized that he wanted to do more than win dance competitions. He decided to start **auditioning** for musicals. He had enjoyed playing the lead role in the musical *Cabaret* while he was in school. Now he wanted to perform in a professional theater production.

> **Derek realized that he wanted to do more than win dance competitions. He decided to start auditioning for musicals.**

Like dance, his theater experiences came with a certain amount of disappointment at first. When Derek auditioned for *Fame: The Musical*, choreographer Karen Bruce appeared to like him. But he did not get the part. A short time later, he tried out for another musical, *Footloose: The Musical*. Once again, Bruce was the **choreographer**. This time she was also the director and had much more say in the casting. She convinced the producers to give Derek the lead role.

He went to work learning his lines and the songs he had to sing in the show. He even took voice lessons to make sure that he could keep up with the demands of performing the show so many times each week. It was especially grueling to do four performances every weekend. In the end all his hard work paid off. The show opened in 2006 and received rave reviews from London theatre **critics**. It also received raves from people whom Derek most wanted to impress—his family. His parents, grandparents, and sisters all flew to London at various times to watch him.

When Derek finished performing *Footloose* a year and a half later, he decided to take a break from performing. Singing and dancing on stage nearly every night had been exhausting. He was tired of the spotlight. But Julianne had another idea. She was preparing to tour as part of *Dancing with the Stars*. Having just concluded its third season, the show was wildly popular in the United States. The tour needed another male dancer for these live performances. Julianne suggested Derek. The idea of spending so much time with his sister appealed to him, so he agreed.

After the tour, Julianne accepted a job as one of the professional dancers on the show for the following season. The producers offered Derek a spot as well. While Derek appreciated the offer, it wasn't what he really wanted to do. He had been living in England for so long that he couldn't imagine moving back to the United States. The Ballases had become like a second family to him. But the situation changed when he found out that Mark Ballas had auditioned for the show. The producers offered Derek a spot again. This time he accepted.

Like many of his other endeavors, Derek started this one despite not feeling entirely ready. "All of a sudden we're on this national stage with millions of people watching and on top of that we're working with celebrities," he told Robyn Ross of *Entertainment Weekly*. "So you have to come in and act like you know what you're doing and act like you're in charge and you're the boss and you're trying to tell this celebrity that you're a fan of how to dance . . . It was like, fake it until you become it."

Derek enjoys making music as well as dancing to it. He performed as a guitarist with the rock band Almost Amy. His friend Mark Ballas was also part of the group.

A Star in His Own Right

Derek rose to the challenge of becoming a dance instructor while the world watched. He also received a great deal of joy from his new role. "I enjoy showing somebody something they really thought they could never do, and you see the confidence build inside," he explained to *Glamour*. "And what it teaches me is that just in everyday life, if you set yourself a challenge that you're going to do something every day, you really can change."

He made his debut on *Dancing with the Stars* in Season Five. It began in late September, 2007. It was not without mishaps. While dancing the quickstep with Jennie Garth, Derek accidentally stepped on his partner's dress. The mistake caused them both to lose their balance and fall. Derek calls the incident his most embarrassing moment on the show. But the pair recovered nicely from this low point. They ended up placing fourth in that season's competition.

By his third season on the show, Derek had found his groove. He and his celebrity partner Brooke Burke won the highly-prized mirror ball trophy in November 2008.

The professional dancers' job on the show involves much more than simply teaching a few moves. Once the contestants get their music, the pros have to choreograph the dance number, design the costumes, teach their partners the steps, and then perform the routine. In his time on the show, Derek won two Emmy awards for his choreography work. In looking back on her victory, Burke told noted entertainment reporter Robin Leach, "He is the most brilliant choreographer ever. He has this way of making his partners look amazing."

The professional halves of the Dancing with the Stars *couples are responsible for planning every part of their performances. Derek won an Emmy award in 2013 for his choreography work on the show.*

In 2014, Derek surprised fans with a dance lesson at the Kellogg's Recharge Bar in New York. The event educated families about the importance of eating a healthy breakfast.

Derek has become one of the world's best-known dancers. He uses his celebrity status to help others. One of his causes is I'm a Dancer Against Cancer. This non-profit organization works to help dancers, dance educators, and choreographers who have been affected by cancer by providing them with financial support and inspiration.

Actress Vanessa Hudgens, who is also part of the charity's celebrity team, knows firsthand how much the support of others can mean in this situation. Her father lost his battle to cancer in 2016. "When someone you love has cancer, it's a very hard thing to deal with for them and for you, but the thing that honestly got me through it was my community that I was surrounded by," she told celebrity blogger Brittany Shawnté.

Whether he is lending his voice to worthy causes like this one or sharing his expertise on the dance floor, Derek leaves a lasting impression with everyone he encounters. Nicole Scherzinger has fond memories of her season on *Dancing with the Stars* because of Derek—and not just because they won the competition. "Derek sees the beauty and the possibility in everything," she said in Derek's memoir. "He is magic and I love him, and the best gift is I won a lifelong friend from that whole experience."

After his sixth *Dancing with the Stars* win, Derek was ready for a new challenge. Instead of returning to the show in 2017, he chose to join several other dance superstars for a new television project called *World of Dance*. Like *Dancing*

In 2017, Derek began a new role with a new dance competition. He is one of the judges on the NBC show World of Dance. *The winner of this contest walks away with a $1 million prize.*

with the Stars, the new show features a panel of judges who rate the performances of a variety of competitors. But this time Derek serves as a judge, not a dancer.

"What makes this dance show different from the rest is that it's global," Derek explained to Jami Ganz of *Entertainment Weekly*. "We're having acts from all over the world come and perform, and there's going to be groups, there's going to be soloists, there's going to be duets and trios, but also, every form of dance you can possibly think of. Probably the biggest difference is that there's an actual prize." The winner of this competition receives one million dollars.

What Derek will do next is anyone's guess. But he is sure to do it with the same passion he has brought to all of his other work as a performer. One of Derek's past *Dancing with the Stars* partners, Kellie Pickler, wrote the foreword for his memoir. "I think whatever the future holds for Derek, he will always be part of something meaningful and that matters," she declared. "There's a big difference between being alive and living—and he's the type of person who believes if you're alive, then you should live to your fullest. I know that there is so much more he will bring to this world—and I can't wait to see it."

> *What Derek will do next is anyone's guess. But he is sure to do it with the same passion he has brought to all of his other work as a performer.*

1985 Derek Hough is born in Salt Lake City, Utah on May 17, 1985.

1997 Derek moves to England to live and study with dance coaches Corky and Shirley Ballas.

2003 He and partner Aneta Piotrowska win the World Under-21 Latin Championships.

2006 Derek lands the lead role in the stage version of the musical film *Footloose* in London.

2007 He joins the cast of *Dancing with the Stars*.

2008 Derek and partner Brooke Burke win Season 7 of *Dancing with the Stars*.

2010 Derek and partner Nicole Scherzinger win Season 10 of *Dancing with the Stars*; he and partner Jennifer Grey win Season 11.

2013 Derek and partner Kellie Pickler win Season 16 of *Dancing with the Stars*; he and partner Amber Riley win Season 17 of *Dancing with the Stars*; Derek wins his first Emmy award for Outstanding Choreography for his work on *Dancing with the Stars*.

2015 Derek wins his second Emmy award for Outstanding Choreography for his work on *Dancing with the Stars*; he wins his sixth *Dancing with the Stars* title with partner Bindi Irwin.

2016 Derek takes part in the *Move Live on Tour* with his sister Julianne; he performs in NBC's musical production *Hairspray Live!*

2017 Derek joins the premiere of *World of Dance* as a judge for the show; he and Julianne go on tour again with their *Move Beyond Live on Tour*.

GLOSSARY

amateur (AM-uh-choor) — a person who practices a hobby, sport, or other pastime for pleasure instead of profit

audition (aw-DISH-uhn) — a trial given to a performer to test his or her ability

awkward (AWK-werd) — lacking ease in social situations

choreographer (kawr-ee-AWG-ruh-fer) — a person who plans the dance steps for a performance

critic (KRIT-ik) — a person who judges a play or other type of artistic performance

eliminate (ih-LIM-uh-neyt) — remove

memoir (MEM-whar) — a person writing about significant events in their life, similar to an autobiography

potential (poe-TEN-shuhl) — an ability within a person that may or may not be developed

technical (TEK-ni-kuhl) — of or relating to technique

verbal (VUR-buhl) — of or relating to words

FURTHER READING

Books

Grayson, Robert. *Dancing with the Stars* (Major Competitive Reality Shows). Broomall, PA: Mason Crest, 2010.

Grimm, R.B. *Derek Hough: Unauthorized and Uncensored.* Kindle edition. Seattle, WA: Amazon Digital Services, 2015

Hough, Derek. *Taking the Lead: Lessons from a Life in Motion.* New York: William Morrow, 2014.

On the Internet

Derek Hough
https://www.derekhough.com/
Move Beyond Live in Tour
https://moveliveontour.com/
World of Dance
http://www.nbc.com/world-of-dance?nbc=1

Works Consulted

———. "Derek Hough." ABC, *Dancing with the Stars.* http://abc.go.com/shows/dancing-with-the-stars/cast/derek-hough

———. "Derek Hough." IMDb. http://www.imdb.com/name/nm2625538/bio

———. "Make Your Move." IMBd. http://www.imdb.com/title/tt1828959/?ref_=nm_flmg_act_7

———. "Move Live on Tour." https://www.moveliveontour.com/news/285533

Aguilera, Leanne. "Dancing With the Stars: Derek Hough Breaks Record With His Fifth Mirror-Ball Victory—Relive His 5 Best Performances." *E News*, November 27, 2013. http://www.eonline.com/news/485884/dancing-with-the-stars-derek-hough-breaks-record-with-his-fifth-mirror-ball-victory-relive-his-5-best-performances

Ganz, Jami. "Derek Hough debuts new music video, talks *World of Dance* $1 million prize." *Entertainment Weekly*, March 28, 2017. http://ew.com/article/2015/11/10/derek-hough-interview/

Grierson, Tim. "The Art of Seizing Opportunity." *Backstage*, November 30, 2016. https://www.backstage.com/interview/art-seizing-opportunity/

King, Brittany. "Derek Hough Reveals His Most Embarrassing *Dancing With The Stars* Moment." *People*, January 4, 2017. http://people.com/tv/derek-hough-reveals-most-embarrassing-dancing-with-stars-moment/

Leach, Robin. "Brooke Burke-Charvet talks husband David Charbet, Derek Hough, L.V." *Las Vegas Sun*, February 29, 2012. https://lasvegassun.com/vegasdeluxe/2012/feb/29/brooke-burke-charvet-talks-husband-david-charvet-d/

Longhetti, Chloe-Lee. "'No joke, she could not dance': Derek Hough reveals Bindi Irwin struggled when she first started Dancing With The Stars." *Daily Mail*, November 21, 2015. http://www.dailymail.co.uk/tvshowbiz/article-3328035/Derek-Hough-reveals-Bindi-Irwin-struggled-started-Dancing-Stars-prepare-finale-practice-AGAIN.html

McNiece, Mia. "Derek And Julianne Hough Open Up About How Their Challenging Childhood Shaped Their Success." *People*, September 23, 2016. http://people.com/celebrity/derek-julianne-hough-open-up-about-how-their-challenging-childhood-shaped-their-success/

Ross, Robyn. "Derek Hough Interview: The *Dancing with the Stars* pro talks about his career." *Entertainment Weekly*, November 10, 2015. http://ew.com/article/2015/11/10/derek-hough-interview/

Shawnté. Brittany. "Vanessa Hudgens, Derek Hough, and More Come Together to Support Dancers Battling Cancer." Celebrities Do Good, May 12, 2016. http://celebritiesdogood.com/2016/05/vanessa-hudgens-derek-hough-celebrities-dancers-against-cancer/

Weinberg, Jen. "DWTS' Derek Hough Says: 'At Times, Teaching People To Dance Is Like Teaching Bambi To Walk On Ice." *Glamour*, February 29, 2012. http://www.glamour.com/story/dwts-derek-hough-says-at-times

INDEX